Published in 2016 by Blue Star Press
Paige Tate & Co. is an Imprint of Blue Star Press
PO Box 8835, Bend, OR 97708
contact@paigetate.com
www.paigetate.com

Printed in Mexico

ISBN: 9781944515287

17 16 15 14 13 12 11 10 9 8

hello! WELCOME TO RELAXATION.

We are so excited to get creative with you!

WE ARE PASSIONATE ABOUT INSPIRING

CREATIVITY

IN EVERYONE. WE SIMPLY PROVIDE THE
BEAUTIFUL CANVAS TO IGNITE THE

COLOR. FRAME. GIVE.

We've created this book with thick paper and perforated edges so that you color these inspirational prints and easily tear them out, frame them, or give them to a friend! The larger prints fit perfectly in an 8 x 10 frame and the smaller prints are the perfect 5 x 7 to frame or mail!

SET *your* MINDS ON THINGS *above*

COLOSSIANS 3:2

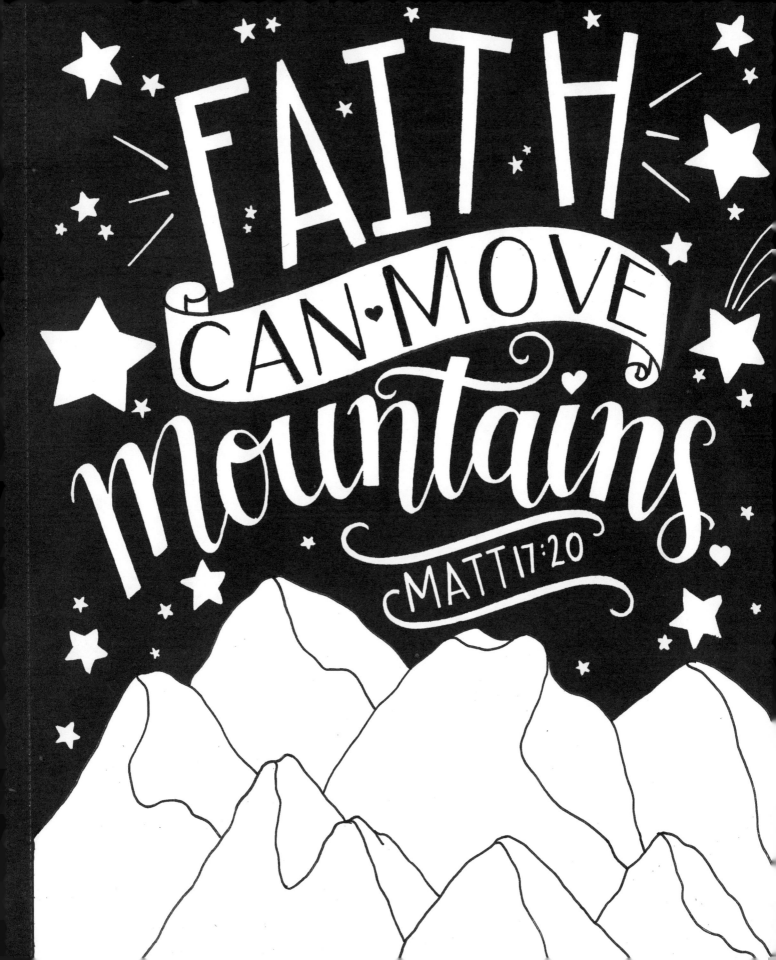

WALK BY faith NOT by Sight

2 COR. 5:7

BE·FULL·of
love·JOY·PEACE
Patience
KINDNESS
Goodness·
FAITHFULNESS
Gentleness·
SELF-CONTROL
GALATIONS 5·22-23

HOPE anchors THE SOUL

HEBREWS 6:19

Fear not, for I am with you. ISAIAH 41:10

AS·FOR·ME

& MY·house

WE·WILL

SERVE

the LORD

JOSHUA 24:15

I can do All things through CHRIST who strengthens ME

-PHIL 4:13-

LET YOUR LIGHT SHINE

MATTHEW 5:16

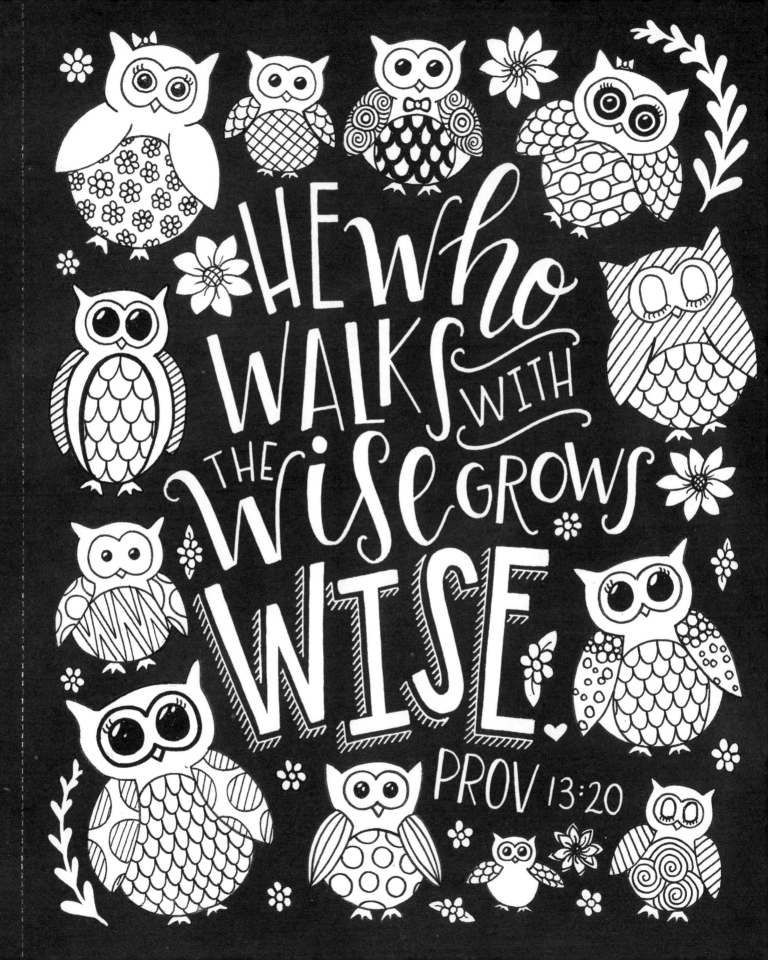

under his wings you will find refuge

PSALM 91:4

FAITH · CAN · MOVE · Mountains · MATT 17:20

MAKE · A · JOYFUL · NOISE · UNTO · the · LORD · PSALM 98:4

Love Never Fails

I COR 13:8

BE FULL OF Love · Joy · Peace · Patience · KINDNESS · Goodness · FAITHFULNESS · Gentleness · SELF-CONTROL

GALATIONS 5:22-23

CHECK OUT OUR BOOKS AT PAIGETATE.COM

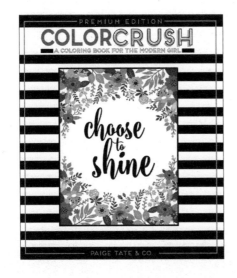

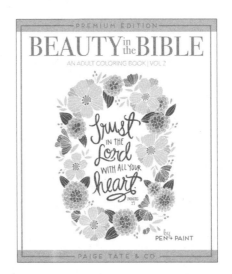

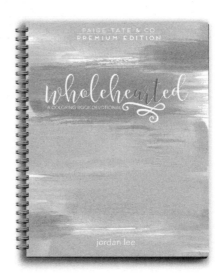

paige tate & co.

www.paigetate.com